TOOLS FOR CAREGIVERS

- **F&P LEVEL:** A
- **WORD COUNT:** 43
- **CURRICULUM CONNECTIONS:** colors

Skills to Teach

- **HIGH-FREQUENCY WORDS:** is, this
- **CONTENT WORDS:** black, blue, brown, bug, gray, green, orange, pink, purple, red, yellow
- **PUNCTUATION:** periods
- **WORD STUDY:** long *a*, spelled *ay* (*gray*); long *e*, spelled *ee* (*green*); long *o*, spelled *ow* (*yellow*); oo sound, spelled *ue* (*blue*); ow sound, spelled *ow* (*brown*); r-controlled vowel (*purple*); short *u*, spelled *u* (*bug*)
- **TEXT TYPE:** information report

Before Reading Activities

- Read the title and give a simple statement of the main idea.
- Have students "walk" though the book and talk about what they see in the pictures.
- Introduce new vocabulary by having students predict the first letter and locate the word in the text.
- Discuss any unfamiliar concepts that are in the text.

After Reading Activities

Have readers review the colors in the Words to Know section on page 2. Practice saying each color out loud as a group. Point out some of the colors they can clearly see around them. Then ask readers to name other objects around them of each color. If there is a color they can't see around them, can they think of something that is that color?

Tadpole Books are published by Jump!, 5357 Penn Avenue South, Minneapolis, MN 55419, www.jumplibrary.com

Copyright ©2020 Jump. International copyright reserved in all countries. No part of this book may be reproduced in any form without written permission from the publisher.

Editor: Jenna Trnka **Designer:** Anna Peterson

Photo Credits: Yellow Cat/Shutterstock, cover; Kletr/Shutterstock, 1; irin-k/Shutterstock, 3; Butterfly Hunter/Shutterstock, 4–5; Marco Uliana/Shutterstock, 6; Jiang Hongyan/Shutterstock, 7; aislutsky/Shutterstock, 8–9, 10; blickwinkel/Alamy, 11; Joesboy/iStock, 12–13; Antagain/iStock, 14; Cristina Romero Palma/Shutterstock, 15; Mark Brandon/Shutterstock, 16.

Library of Congress Cataloging-in-Publication Data
Names: Peterson, Anna C., 1982– author.
Title: Let's learn colors / by Anna C. Peterson.
Other titles: Let us learn colors
Description: Tadpole books. | Minneapolis: Jump!, Inc., (2020) | Series: Fun first concepts
"Tadpole Books are published by Jump!" | Audience: Ages 3–6.
Identifiers: LCCN 2019032821 (print) | LCCN 2019032822 (ebook) | ISBN 9781645273110 (hardcover)
ISBN 9781645273127 (paperback) | ISBN 9781645273134 (ebook)
Subjects: LCSH: Colors—Juvenile literature. | Color—Juvenile literature. | Vocabulary.
Classification: LCC QC495.5 .P477567 2020 (print) | LCC QC495.5 (ebook) | DDC 535.6—dc23
LC record available at https://lccn.loc.gov/2019032821
LC ebook record available at https://lccn.loc.gov/2019032822

FUN FIRST CONCEPTS

LET'S LEARN COLORS

by Anna C. Peterson

TABLE OF CONTENTS

tadpole
books

WORDS TO KNOW

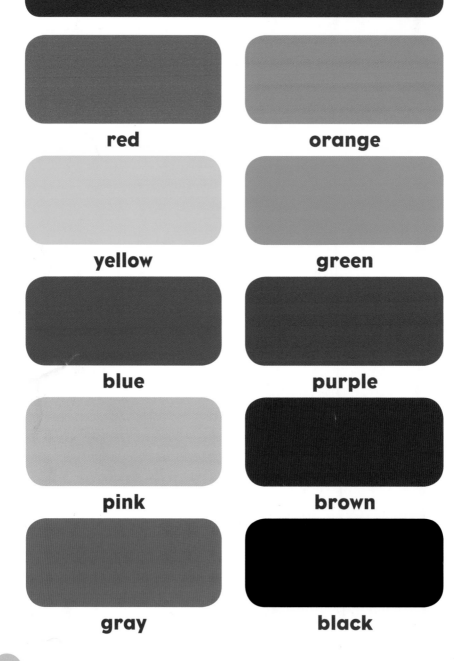

red

orange

yellow

green

blue

purple

pink

brown

gray

black

LET'S LEARN COLORS!

ladybug ····▶

This bug is red.

butterfly

This bug is orange.

wasp

This bug is yellow.

grasshopper

This bug is green.

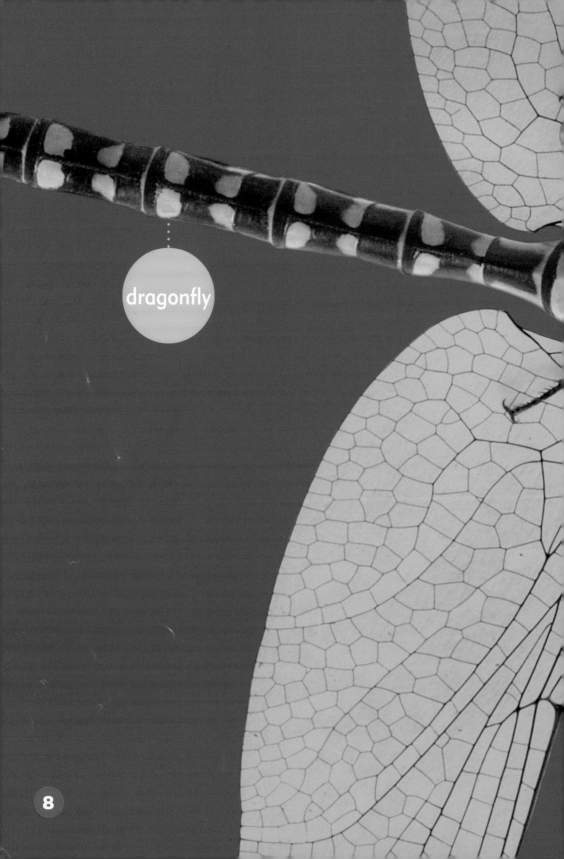

dragonfly

This bug is blue.

beetle

This bug is purple.

mantis

This bug is pink.

stink bug

This bug is brown.

silverfish

This bug is gray.

ant

This bug is black.

LET'S REVIEW!

What colors do you see on this bug?

INDEX